HOW WE
LIVE NOW

BY THE SAME AUTHOR

How New York Breaks Your Heart
Insomniac City: New York, Oliver, and Me
The Anatomist: A True Story of Gray's Anatomy
Sleep Demons: An Insomniac's Memoir
Five Quarts: A Personal and Natural History of Blood

HOW WE LIVE NOW

BILL HAYES

SCENES FROM THE PANDEMIC

BLOOMSBURY PUBLISHING

NEW YORK · LONDON · OXFORD · NEW DELHI · SYDNEY

BLOOMSBURY PUBLISHING
Bloomsbury Publishing Inc.
1385 Broadway, New York, NY 10018, USA

BLOOMSBURY, BLOOMSBURY PUBLISHING, and the Diana logo are trademarks
of Bloomsbury Publishing Plc

First published in the United States 2020

ISBN: HB: 978-1-63557-688-7
          eBook: 978-1-63557-689-4

Library of Congress Cataloging-in-Publication Data is available

2 4 6 8 10 9 7 5 3 1

Typeset by Westchester Publishing Services
Printed and bound in the U.S.A. by Berryville Graphics Inc., Berryville, Virginia

To find out more about our authors and books visit www.bloomsbury.com and
sign up for our newsletters.

Bloomsbury books may be purchased for business or promotional use. For information
on bulk purchases please contact Macmillan Corporate and Premium Sales Department
at specialmarkets@macmillan.com.

For Nancy Miller,
and in memory of Wendy Weil

Of course, it was hard not to worry, everyone was worried, but it wouldn't do to panic, because, as Max pointed out to Quentin, there wasn't anything one could do except wait and hope, wait and start being careful, be careful and hope . . .

—Susan Sontag, from "The Way We Live Now," 1986

1

It is one year ago, and I am walking up Hudson Street near where I live:

I cross paths with a beautifully dressed young man with a long, pitch-black beard, and I ask if I can take his picture. He demurs immediately.

But we go on chatting. He tells me he's a writer from Turkey, here to look for stories.

"So, have you found any?"

"Yes, this is a story now," he replies, with a sideways glance.

I laugh. "For me, too."

We shake hands and I tell him my name.

"I'm Yevgeny," he says, and begins walking ahead of me at a faster clip. "Good day now."

"Good day, Yevgeny."

Tango Dancers at the Pier
July 10, 2019

2

Now, I think about:

The last time I shook hands with a stranger.
The last time I saw people dancing.
The last time I saw people smiling.
The last time I heard kids playing.
The last time I saw traffic on Eighth Avenue.
The last time I went to the gym.
The last time I went swimming.
The last time I took the subway.
The last time I took a plane.
The last time I went to a movie.
The last time I went to a play.
The last time I made someone laugh.
The last time I made someone dinner.
The last time I kissed someone.
The last time I slept with someone.
The last time I fucked someone.
The last time I let someone fuck me.

The last time I shared a joint.

The last time I took a taxi.

The last time I took an Uber.

The last time I took a bus.

The last time I went to a restaurant.

The last time I went to brunch.

The last time I went to a grocery store without fear.

The last time I got a haircut.

The last time I got a drink at a bar.

The last time I took a bath with someone.

The last time I saw food carts on Fourteenth Street.

The last time I saw a crowded sidewalk.

The last time I saw people sitting on their stoops.

The last time I saw Ali at the smoke shop.

The last time I saw anyone in my family.

The last time I saw friends in person.

The last time I saw Hailey.

The last time I saw my therapist at his office.

The last time I heard cars honking.

The last time I shared an elevator without worrying.

The last time I went outside without a mask or gloves.

The last time I wasn't scared.

The last time I was as scared as this.

The last time I fell in love.

Eighth Avenue
December 10, 2019

3

It was Christmas, just last Christmas—the last time I fell in love. It was a temporary condition, true, but that doesn't make it any less real. I am and always have been a love-at-first-sight kind of human.

I had made a deliberate decision to approach the holidays this time not as *the holidays*—which had made me blue for years—but just as work days. I had a project to keep me fully occupied, fortunately. I worked all day on Christmas and had no plans to go out. If someone had invited me to a Christmas dinner, say, I would have said no, no thank you. But by six, I was feeling restless and I decided to take a walk.

I wandered through the West Village, passed by a bar on Christopher Street, then, on second thought, turned around and went in to check it out. I was sure it would be empty—six thirty on Christmas night, come on—but it was not. There were lots of people there, mostly people like me, I guessed, which is to say people who don't dig the holidays or believe in Jesus and don't have family here or a menorah or a Christmas tree. To my relief, old-school disco, not Christmas music, was playing. I ordered a Corona and a shot of tequila—my way of celebrating a good day's work—and settled in on a barstool. I didn't plan to stay for long.

Sometime later—let's say another beer later—the guy on the stool next to me talked me into playing a game of pool.

"The last time I played pool I was in high school forty years ago," I warned him, but of course that was all the more reason for him to take me on. He beat me in what must have been record time—even for that bar, not known for pool sharks—which meant a round of drinks was on me. That's when I spotted Jesse. He was leaning against the back wall. He was tall and muscular, but it was the Santa hat he wore with exactly the right amount of irony that caught my eye. Somehow it made him even handsomer. And then he smiled. I'm a sucker for a gap-toothed smile, I just am. He held my gaze and just kept smiling this sexy, gap-toothed grin.

The bartender returned with the beers I'd ordered. "One for him, too," I said, gesturing at the tall young Black Santa with the irresistible lips. "Whatever he's drinking, tell him it's on me."

He came over and thanked me and asked if he could play pool, too. "Teams—we'll do teams," he suggested.

"You do not want me on your team," I said.

"Yeah, I, uh, I picked up on that," he said.

He found another guy to be his pool partner and we played more games than I clearly remember. My guy and I lost each one, that I do know. Somewhere in there, maybe after someone had bought the first round of shots, Jesse and I exchanged phone numbers. The chemistry between us, with alcohol speeding up the process, was palpable. I remember thinking, *This is the most fun I've had on Christmas in I do not know how long.*

But then things started to get fuzzy. I can drink—up to a point—but the last thing I wanted was to get wasted. I decided I had to get myself back home while I still had my wits about me. So I split. I put my pool cue aside and, with no goodbyes, slipped out the door. It was only about nine thirty or ten. The fresh, cold air felt bracing, sobering. I was halfway home when I got a text:

"What happened to you? Where are you?" It was Jesse.

"On my way home, time for bed," I texted.

There was no response for a couple blocks, then: "Bed? This is where you're supposed to invite me over," he texted back.

Oh, right. *Right.* I did a quick calculation, weighing the pros and cons, and within a few seconds, *What the hell, it is Christmas after all* won the argument in my head. I texted him my address.

Those long legs of his got him to my place in half the time it had taken me. I'd barely had time to brush my teeth when my doorbell rang: There was Jesse leaning against the door frame, still wearing his Santa hat and now with a string of Christmas lights around his neck.

"I swiped these on the way out," he said.

"I like your style, let's find a place to plug them in," I said.

4

One of the realities of living in New York is that you cannot become too attached to specific places any more than you can become attached to certain people in your life: the waitress you chat with every weekend, the parking garage guy, the newsstand vendor from whom you buy a paper. Often, they disappear, and you may never learn why. Why did that bar close so suddenly? Whatever happened to their bartender? And what about Mohammed? He was here yesterday.

We have always known this, those of us who've lived in New York a while.

What's happening in the city now, though, is that it's not just one or two people you notice have gone missing. It feels like it's everyone. Everywhere. Except for a few people remaining in a few places—the gas station guys, the liquor store, the pharmacy—everyone has disappeared.

My apartment building, where I'm sequestered by myself at my place, is less than half full. Many residents have moved to their second homes in the Hamptons or upstate; some younger ones have gone back home to live with their parents. There are no children left in this entire eighteen-story building. One of my neighbors on another floor, Margo, died from Covid-19 a few days ago. Almost every day, I hear about someone else who's gotten it.

In the past week alone, I've seen the city itself change before my eyes from my apartment windows. In the daytime, Eighth Avenue—stretching from Fourteenth Street to Central Park South, nearly fifty city blocks—is so empty that couples are walking hand in hand down the middle of the street. Skateboarders and bicyclists ride where cars used to be.

It's lovely in a certain, dreamlike way. But then I notice the surgical masks on faces, the distance between pedestrians, and I have to look away. It's just not right. It's just not right. I lie down.

Eighth Avenue
April 6, 2020

5

As the days pass, one blurring into another, I find I often wonder what my late partner, the British-born neurologist and author Oliver Sacks, would say. Had he lived to see this, Oliver would be in what we now know is one of the most vulnerable categories: the elderly. (He'd be eighty-six today.) Oliver was also, by his own admission, a hypochondriac, a prodigious hand-washer and nail-scrubber long before it became de rigueur. But then, he'd also lived through the Blitz, and AIDS, and 9/11; as a young doctor, he'd treated survivors of the encephalitis lethargica pandemic that swept the world in the early twentieth century, killing or incapacitating five million people—his *Awakenings* patients, as they'd come to be known. And he had faced his own impending death from cancer with uncommon grace and clarity. So I am pretty sure I know what his response would be. A few months before he died at eighty-two in August 2015, Oliver looked up from his notepad one evening——in this apartment, while sitting at this desk—and said the following to me:

The most we can do is to write—intelligently, creatively, critically, evocatively—about what it is like living in the world at this time.

Oliver was a man of many enthusiasms but none more so than for the power and poetry of words. When I say he loved words, I don't simply mean within the context of being a writer of numerous classic books. Even if he had never written a single one, I am sure Oliver would still have been that funny fellow who took giant dictionaries to bed for light reading (aided by a magnifying glass). He delighted in etymology, synonyms and antonyms, slang, swear words, palindromes, anatomical terms, neologisms. He could joyfully parse the difference between homonyms and homophones, not to mention homographs, in dinner table conversation.

It was this love of words and of the act of writing—which he considered a form of thinking—that led Oliver to tell me one day shortly after I'd moved to New York in the spring of 2009, "You *must* keep a journal!"

It was not a suggestion but an instruction.

I followed his advice straightaway, writing that exchange down on a scrap of paper, which I still have with me. I hadn't kept a journal since I was a teenager, but I began chronicling impressions of life in New York and of my encounters with people I'd meet by chance on the street or subway—a practice I have continued to this day.

Oliver at Home
March 6, 2015

6

As with Christmas, I had made no plans for New Year's Eve this year. I just worked that day and expected to work the next day too. Unlike Christmas, however, New Year's is a holiday I kind of like—a chance to put one year behind you and to celebrate what-may-be, 365 days open to all possibilities. I felt optimistic. Two major writing projects I'd been working on—one of which I'd spent a decade on—would be coming to fruition over the next six months. I'd also completed a new body of photographic work and looked forward to editing down the pictures and possibly putting together a show. If nothing else, I would pour a glass of wine before midnight on the thirty-first and watch TV and toast to new beginnings.

But then I got a text from Jesse. His plans for the night had fallen through and he wondered what I was up to.

"Having a date with myself," I texted.

"How about I join you?"

He arrived around ten thirty. I took his backpack for him as he took off his coat; it was unusually heavy. He unzipped it and pulled out a magnum of sparkling rosé.

"Are you shittin' me?" I said with a chuckle, already imagining the hangover this much sweet wine could bring. But I was touched, truth be told. The last time I'd celebrated New Year's Eve with someone was with Oliver. Jesse popped the cork, I plugged the Christmas lights back in, and we got our little party started. I had to take a shelf out of my refrigerator just to accommodate that bottle of rosé, large enough for a party of six.

We smoked a joint and lost track of time but were in bed before midnight. The only reason I know this for sure is because, seemingly by chance, we both happened to glance at my clock at the exact moment it turned from 11:59 to 12:00—from 2019 to 2020. We looked at each other, our mouths agape. "Oh my God," we said in unison, and then we kissed. And kissed. And kissed. A flush of good feeling washed over me, a sensation I remember clearly; it was almost like having a premonition: *The year ahead is going to be such a joyful one.*

Boy, did I get that wrong.

7

It's strange to try to retrace one's steps, thinking about where you were at what point in this pandemic while still in the *midst* of this pandemic—and whether or not you'd ever been or had put yourself at risk. Things have changed so quickly in such a short time. I look at my 2020 calendar now and I can see—by the various appointments and dates on it (I obsessively write everything down)—how I, like most everyone else on the planet, was living as if everything were perfectly normal throughout all of January and February: going to the gym, going for a mile-long swim, going out with friends, going to therapy, going out for dinner, going to the doctor, and so forth. How oblivious I was. How oblivious we all were to how your entire life can change in a few days.

8

The last time I traveled by plane was in late November. The film-maker Ric Burns had completed a powerful full-length documentary about Oliver's life and work, which was screening at a festival in Los Angeles. I joined one of the producers for a post-screening Q-and-A at a theater right off the Hollywood Walk of Fame. We had a full house, and I looked forward to doing more—screenings at festivals scheduled throughout the spring, one in Martha's Vineyard in March, for which I already had flight tickets, one in Portland, Oregon, and others. But by March, the year's remaining film festivals had been canceled and movie theaters were shutting down. I wondered if and when I would ever travel again, and why—why would I want to?

Even under the best circumstances, travel can be a grind—the lines, the waits, security; long, crowded flights, crammed into economy. But I've always enjoyed the trip to and from the airport; each provides a different form of anticipation. Whereas on a plane I feel like human cargo, in a long cab or Uber ride with a skilled driver, I feel like a *passenger*, free of any responsibilities, free to daydream or doze if I like or to strike up a conversation, if the vibe is right. A certain driver on a certain night a few years ago comes back to me now as a welcome reminder.

Here's the situation: We are stuck in heavy traffic on the way to JFK. I'm getting out of town for a few days. Running late—more bored than stressed—I lean forward and ask the driver what his plans are for the night.

"Sleep. Get some sleep," he says. "Haven't slept three nights—"

"Three nights is rough—what's going on?"

He looks at me in the rearview mirror, black circles under his eyes: "I'm in love."

"You're in love?"

He nods.

"What a good reason for insomnia."

He half-smiles. "Yeah, but . . . I got such a bad headache—my whole head."

Love'll do that, I say to myself.

"So, is she here?" I ask. "Is this why you're not sleeping—like, she's in your bed and you're not used to that, or—?"

"—No, no, we just met, or re-met—two weeks maybe, back home; just got back a couple days ago. Crazy, man. Didn't expect it. I've known her family so long. I'm thirty-five . . ." His voice trailed off.

Funny: He'd listed three excellent conditions for falling in love, it seemed to me, not for it to be unexpected.

"Where's home?" I ask.

"Pakistan."

Traffic begins to move. He shifts out of Park. We ride for a while in silence.

"People there—they're more reserved than here," he says, picking up his story. "Stuff like this, love at first sight—it's crazy, man, it doesn't happen . . ."

"Not crazy, trust me—I'm a veteran." The driver glances back at me, and I ask, "So, what's next? You go back there, or . . . ?"

"No, I bring her here, to New York—on a fiancée visa."

I have never heard of this but I'm glad such a thing exists. I wonder if two men can do that, or two women? A fiancée visa; I should look into that.

"Congratulations," I say, "I'm Billy, by the way, what's your name?"

"Abdul."

I give Abdul my card and say I'd love to come to the wedding if there is room.

"I'll take photos," I say.

Couple in Love
August 8, 2019

Girl in a White Dress
Gay Pride Day, June 30, 2019

Woman Alone on a Park Bench
March 21, 2020

9

I can see already how photography can document the rapidity with which things are changing, and equally, how street photography as I've practiced it may never be the same. I first started taking pictures seriously just after moving here. I bought a good camera and taught myself how to use it; I'd always wanted to take pictures. But that didn't make me a photographer. New York—that is, New Yorkers who were open to allowing a complete stranger to take quick portraits of them on the spot—made me a photographer. I've taken tens of thousands of pictures—the kinds of pictures I may never be able to capture again: happy, sweaty throngs at street fairs and parades; sunbathers, frisbee-players, stoop-sitters; unlikely lineups of characters crowded onto park benches in every pocket of the city.

New York at night is a whole different landscape too. A photo I took in December of a traffic-clogged Eighth Avenue on a typical evening around six: that sea of red lights— what I once described as a "fiery red Milky Way on the streets of Manhattan"—is simply not there to be shot anymore. When I look out my window at night now, Eighth Avenue looks like a sky snuffed of its stars.

On the other hand, with the absence of traffic comes other things, things I had not noticed before. In place of the brilliant red stoplights and traffic lights that lit up at the same time at certain times from here till Central Park, now it's the green lights—one, two, three, four, and on—I look for. Often nowadays there are only two or three drivers down there. I stand at my window and watch them hit all the green lights without ever having to stop, from here to what seems like infinity. That must be such a good feeling. I almost want to clap or cheer. Or weep. I'm not sure why I find this so moving, until another thought comes to mind, a far scarier one, like something out of sci-fi: *What if I looked out and saw no cars at all?* Not one. As if every last person in Manhattan were taken by this pandemic except for me, standing alone up here.

10

Life after life after death: that's how I've come to think of this post-Oliver period. Oddly enough, it was easier in the beginning—the first couple of years. I had a lot to do, that was key: memorials and tributes to help plan; his book-filled apartment to clean out and organize; new collections of Oliver's work to co-edit and help see through publication posthumously; and, not least, two books of my own to write and photograph. But as things finally quieted down, at the beginning of 2018, depression descended.

When you're really depressed, the last thing you want to talk about is your depression. And yet at the same time you're dying to be asked about it. I felt embarrassed that I had not bounced back—in fact, had fallen back many steps—that I still struggled with paralyzing loneliness and sadness. People close to me probably did not know this. I'm sure friends and family assumed I was doing okay. I rarely said otherwise or, if I did, I sometimes felt shut down, dismissed.

I remember catching up with a friend I had not seen in three years. He asked how I was doing and I said, "I think my heart is permanently broken, or at least irreparably cracked." Maybe I even said it with a smile, self-consciously, but I was trying to give him a sense of how damaged I felt.

"Come on, you'll be *fine*! I think your heart's just exhausted."

How could he, a happily married man who'd never lost a partner or spouse, be so sure? I certainly wasn't. I just looked at him and nodded.

Maybe it was an accumulation of losses: Not only my partner, but both my parents as well as my literary agent, who was a mentor and a one-of-a-kind New York character, all in the last several years.

Maybe it was New York City—a place I fell in love with when I moved here, but one whose far tougher side I'd gotten to know recently. It can be a lonely place, New York, a hard place to make friends, especially in middle age.

Or maybe it *was* me—a distinct possibility. Maybe my friend did get it right: maybe I was exhausted—metaphorically and literally.

I've never been a good sleeper, but around that time my insomnia became so intractable I went for a consultation at a sleep disorders clinic in Manhattan, hoping for some silver bullet. Dr. Lamb was as kindly and gentle as his surname implies. After doing a physical exam, hearing my whole story and medical history, carefully typing it all into his computer, he looked at me with grave concern and said, "All of the medications you're taking—the antidepressants, anti-anxiety meds, sleeping pills—if you ever mix them with alcohol, well, that can be very dangerous. Deadly. That's how people like Marilyn Monroe died."

I just stared back at him, my entire body filling with shame like a glass left under a running faucet.

"Those drugs were all prescribed by doctors," I said defensively, "it's not as if I bought them on the street."

He nodded sympathetically, then added, "Here's my concern: This is where you're at at fifty-seven. But where will you be in ten years? Where will you be at sixty-seven?"

Sitting in his cozy consultation office, I could not imagine why my presence on this planet at age sixty-seven would matter at all. I did not care if I lived or died.

Even so, I took his words seriously—primarily because he, this stranger, this sleep doctor whom I would never see again, seemed so concerned about me. With guidance from my own physician, I eliminated most of the medications I'd been on and cut way back on alcohol. I got into therapy, too—weekly talk therapy, which has probably helped more than anything else. I've been seeing the same therapist for the past two and a half years (now via Zoom).

The most important thing I've learned about depression is not to think about it as "a depression," as if it were a single monolithic thing. There are many parts to it, built up over time, perhaps a lifetime—grief, trauma, abuse, isolation, rejection, resentment, financial stress, professional setbacks, etc. But if you can zero in on and break off even just one distinct part—to tell your truth, every word of it—your load lightens considerably.

Women in White
July 17, 2019

11

I bought lightweight leather gloves to wear for extra protection on the subway (I got workout gloves for the gym, too). I carried a small bottle of hand sanitizer with me. I'd never been a germophobe by any means, but, even when there were fewer than fifty Covid-related deaths reported in New York in early March, I had a feeling that subway cars, packed with straphangers and ideal vectors for viral transmission, were going to be places I'd want to avoid. (My first job in New York was working for a global nonprofit that was working on developing an AIDS vaccine; I'd learned a great deal about how viruses work and about human immunology and vaccinology.)

The last time I took a subway was on March 13. I was on my way to pick up some of my photographs, which I'd had printed and framed at a small business in Long Island City. I suppose I could have taken an Uber or cab, but why? The subway was cheap and fast, and stopped just two blocks from my destination. The rides back and forth to the frame shop were uneventful, but the mood inside the subway cars was tense. People were not yet wearing masks and only a few wore gloves like me, but everyone was doing their best to keep as far away from everyone else as possible. More people stood than sat, bunched together, for example—a rarity; you could practically get tackled for a spare seat in earlier times. This is not how New York, the New York I knew, operated.

I remembered being on an uptown 4/5 train one evening at the height of rush hour. If you have never been on an uptown 4/5 train at the height of rush hour, you can't imagine just how jampacked it can get. The air you are breathing, the warmth you are feeling, the scent you are smelling, is not your own but a mix of everybody's. Sometimes it is so crowded you can't even grab a pole to hang on to; you remain wedged tightly among other riders, shoulder to shoulder, ass to ass. There's no chance you'd fall over even if you wanted to.

On this particular evening, I am stuck in my least favorite spot: standing in the middle of a row, nowhere near either door, so getting myself out of here is going to be a polite-as-possible, but not *too* polite, push-and-shove maneuver. At least I am able to hang on to an overhead pole. The car is pretty quiet, which is typical—people generally keep to themselves on the subway—at least at first.

Suddenly, a young woman starts singing—she has headphones on—*really* singing, loudly. I can see her through the crowd. She faces the door, watches her reflection in the glass, and sings her heart out. She isn't busking. I wonder if she is on her way to an audition, practicing her big number for a new Broadway show?

Suddenly, she stops. "I'm sorry for the noise!" she yells loudly enough for everyone in the entire car to hear.

All the passengers around her shake their heads, shrug: *No, not noise.*

"I've heard way worse," the man next to me says.

An L Train at Rush Hour, 5:05 P.M.
April 22, 2020

Fourteenth Street Station, 4:45 P.M.
April 16, 2020

1 2

I've done some dating the past few years, not much but some. I gave it a concerted effort with two guys in particular before Jesse, good guys, both around my age, but neither relationship lasted more than two months. Maybe I never wanted to date in the first place, it strikes me now. What I wanted was romance. Electricity. The kind of electricity I felt when I moved to New York. Or when I first met Oliver. Or any time Jesse walked through the door.

We saw each other throughout January and February, and into March. It hadn't evolved into a full-fledged relationship, in part because we were both busy, I with my work and Jesse not only with two different jobs but also with school—he was pursuing a degree full-time at a Manhattan college. There were other reasons too, the dominant one being that there was—there is—a huge age difference between us: I'm fifty-nine. He's twenty-six (soon to be twenty-seven, a birthday I won't be able to celebrate with him in person for obvious reasons).

I know something about age gaps, about so-called intergenerational relationships: After all, Oliver was twenty-eight years older than me. But this felt different: it wasn't just that Jesse was much younger than me; I felt I was too old for him—too used to my routines, to doing my own thing. To being alone. The truth is, though, we rarely talked about our age difference. We'd see each other about once a week, maybe more if it worked out. We always had a good time, getting stoned, making dinner (and breakfast the next morning), having sex, taking baths together in my big tub, watching TV, hanging out, laughing. He made me laugh, and I him, which I loved and appreciated. I hadn't laughed so much with someone in five years.

And then the pandemic hit.

In New York, the mandate to practice social distancing of at least six feet came in mid-March, so that made continuing a casual relationship such as ours challenging, if not risky. His college, where a few Covid cases had been identified in students, was shut down. Large gatherings of any kind were discouraged. Businesses had to close by eight P.M. Some were already closing for good. On the same day, Jesse lost both his jobs—one at a downtown gym, where he worked at the front desk, and one as a bouncer at an East Village bar, where he had to be in contact with hundreds of people. And for my own work, I'd often been out on the streets photographing complete strangers all over the place. We couldn't know whether we'd been exposed somehow, could we?

"I don't think we're supposed to see each other, to be near each other," I had to say to Jesse when he said he was heading over to my place that night.

"Nah, come on, we're fine."

"No, I don't think we *know* if we're fine, I don't think we should, not yet."

But gradually, with each text exchanged, my resistance weakened: "Okay, come over, but we can't have sex."

He agreed. But after doing our best to keep away from each other at either end of the couch, our willpower broke and we started making out.

I don't regret it; on the contrary, I treasure it—that memory. Already, that seems like a different life, just over one month ago. We didn't know exactly what was going on, whom to believe, everything was happening very fast. Everyone was talking about handwashing (how many demonstrations of the proper handwashing method by celebrities did I watch on social media?). No one was saying anything about sex.

And then there was that big beautiful tattooed Trinidadian man with the sexy smile for me to consider. What can I say? Desire is a powerful force to tamp down.

We had a blast that night, and the next day, but there was something bittersweet about it too, and something missing: a certain carefreeness. I knew this would most likely be the last time in a while I'd see Jesse, touch him, be with him. *Be* with him, in the deepest sense of that phrase—our lives as intertwined as our bodies at this odd moment in time. Be with anyone.

The Last Time I Kissed a Man
March 14, 2020, 1:44 P.M.

1 3

A disruption in the universe, I jotted in my journal on Thursday, March 17. I couldn't think of any other way to put it. Words had begun to seem insufficient.

I took a walk and took a photo of waves crashing violently in the Hudson: that seemed to capture things more accurately.

I made a to-do list:

- Clean toilet
- Clean desk
- Clean file drawers
- Clean closets
- Clean oven
- Clean whole apartment
- Inventory O's books
- Refill prescriptions
- Call Kathy
- Call Yolanda
- Call Jane
- Go to therapy

- Take a walk
- Read during the day
- Create home exercise routine
- Buy groceries
- Buy weed
- Buy wine
- Buy disinfectant
- Buy masks
- Stop taking your temperature

14

I was just about to take my daily pills when it hit me for the first time today that I might as well put one of the tablets back into the bottle: the light-blue one, Truvada, a medication that prevents HIV infection in people who are HIV-negative and sexually active; it's commonly known as PreP (Pre-exposure Prophylaxis).

"I'm not gonna be needing you for now," I murmured, plucking it from my palm. As a single person without a partner or spouse, I'm not going to be having sex with anyone anytime soon as long as coronavirus remains a threat and widespread testing is nonexistent.

Am I sad about that? You bet. Am I looking for sympathy? No. But it did serve as a reckoning quite distinct from handwashing, working from home, disinfecting surfaces, and other measures recommended by public health officials. Talk about social distancing: For millions like me—male, female, and nonbinary; gay, straight, bi, trans, and queer—staying healthy during this pandemic also includes being celibate. We don't know how long we'll have to live like this—like Catholic priests or nuns who actually keep their vows.

Before my light-blue pill and I parted ways, I took a moment to reflect. I'm grateful to it—to the scientists who developed it; to the clinical trial volunteers who helped to test it—for keeping me healthy. Not only physically but mentally healthy. Since I started on PreP a few years ago, I've been able to enjoy a sex life freer from fear of HIV infection than any I'd known since I was in my early twenties.

I appreciate down to my blood and bones and balls what it took, the time it took, the expense it took, the toll it took—everything and everyone it took—to develop antiviral drugs like this one and, even more, the medications that can now keep people with HIV or AIDS alive and healthy, their virus "undetectable."

I remember as if it were yesterday what it was like when there was nothing—and I mean *nothing*—to treat HIV/AIDS, much less to prevent it (something I truly thought I'd never see). Screw that. I remember what it was like when we didn't even know what caused the nightmarish illness that at first mainly struck gay men, rendering them mortally ill in weeks, gone within months. I remember when the mysterious virus—Human Immunodeficiency Virus, as it was named—was identified at last in 1983, and when the modes of transmission into the bloodstream were finally made explicitly clear (unprotected sexual intercourse, whether vaginal or anal, and injection drug use being the riskiest). I remember when some of the first drugs to treat AIDS were introduced and tested— they were almost as toxic as ingesting disinfectants. And I remember the day—the moment—when I fell in love with a twenty-six-year-old named Steve, who told me on our first date that he had tested HIV-positive. I was twenty-eight and had tested HIV-negative. This was in 1989. Soon after, I moved in with him. We were together, a "mixed-status couple," as such couples were known, for almost seventeen years. Steve died unexpectedly, not from AIDS, paradoxically, but from a heart attack at age forty-three. He was in bed next to me when I woke to find him in cardiac arrest. EMTs came, but it was too late. It's been almost fourteen years since that morning in October but I still think about him, still have dreams about him, still remember the last words we spoke. They were not *goodbye*. There were no goodbyes. We were in bed the night before, reading, around eleven or so. I decided to turn in first and shut off my light.

"Good night," I said and kissed him on the lips.

"Good night," Steve said, "I'm just gonna read a couple more pages."

1 5

Delivery Biker at a Red Light

I took his picture just as
the light turned green
and he began riding off.

"What's your name?"
I called
as I got out of the way.

He turned his head and said—
said it—
as he rode away.

But I couldn't hear.
I watched him disappear
up the avenue.

16

Yesterday, feeling fine physically but going stir-crazy in my apartment, I decided to take a walk. It was a beautiful afternoon in New York, after all, and taking a walk is still permitted. My hour-long walk—winding through the West Village, down to the Hudson, and by the river—was mind-clearing. I headed home via Christopher Street. Nearly everything was closed, of course. But balancing out the spookiness of the deserted streets and all the shuttered restaurants, bars, and shops were the sweetly worded handwritten signs posted by small business owners—expressing thanks to loyal customers, wishing everyone well, and promising to "be back soon."

On a whim, I decided to extend my walk and see if Three Lives & Company was open. Although I happen to have thousands of Oliver's books in storage in my apartment—any one of which might be fascinating—somehow, I felt I needed a *new* book. I suppose I wanted to give myself a little gift, but I also wanted to see how my local booksellers were faring.

There's no way they'll be open, I thought to myself, *it's such a tiny shop*. Alas, as I approached, I saw that the bookshop looked dark inside, no lights on. Ah, but then I noticed, from half a block away, the door was open . . .

. . . An old wooden chair, propping open the door, blocked entry into the shop. *How sad—maybe they're closing for good and packing up?* But no. I peeked my head in and there were Miriam and Troy, stalwarts of independent booksellers, smiles on their faces. We greeted one another with cheer and affection, and Miriam explained how they'd adjusted things: No one was allowed inside—Troy was sequestered behind the counter and Miriam was standing halfway between him and the entrance—but if you'd "Just call out the title of the book" you were looking for (or the author, or the genre), they'd find it for you. And they did! I had specific titles in mind—a big thick book called *The Dolphin Letters* about Robert Lowell, Elizabeth Hardwick, and others of their literary circle—and the new Rebecca Solnit memoir, which I was eager to read. Miriam went in search.

Behind me a small line had formed. I stepped aside. One woman called out for "the new Hilary Mantel, please!" (They had a towering stack of those.) A couple was seeking "a new cookbook—anything you suggest?" (Between them, Miriam and Troy had a bunch of creative ideas.) A family was looking for books for their little kids to read. I felt like I was in a metaphorical breadline—a breadline for feeding the brain and the soul.

Miriam placed my books on the old wooden chair propping open the door after I'd taken a few steps back, and then I picked them up with my begloved hands.

"Should I toss my credit card in, or leave it on the chair here?" I asked.

"No," Miriam told me—they were being very strict about social distancing, she explained. "Just read out the numbers on your credit card—Troy will ring it up!" she called back.

And so I did, yelling out my VISA numbers unselfconsciously. Troy, thoughtful as always, asked if I wanted a receipt or a bag?

"No, no, I'm happy to carry them," I replied.

And I was. The big thick book and Rebecca's memoir felt so good in my hand—substantial, weighty, as if they were heavy simply because of the promise of several days and nights of reading ahead. I bid goodbye as Miriam and Troy took care of the other neighbors.

"We're going to try to stay open as long as we can—as long as it's safe and we're permitted," Miriam said.

I wished them well with all my heart: I felt I had gotten many gifts on this outing, not just one. "Bless you both," I said.

Young Woman on Fourteenth Street
August 6, 2018

1 7

I had a dream about Oliver, one of the few I've had since he died: I see him opening the door to the coat closet in the apartment. He has his shirt off and his soft pajama trousers on. It seems as if he is looking for something that's gone missing, as he often was, and I hear him murmuring softly to himself:

". . . Now where *is* it . . . ?"

I come up from behind and wrap him in a big hug, startling him—"*Oh!*" But he realizes it is me, and even though I can't see his face, I can feel Oliver smiling. His body goes from tensed to relaxed in my arms. He keeps looking for whatever he was looking for, reaching up to the top shelf, while I keep hugging him.

". . . The important thing is stay *active*," Oliver says.

I run a hand over his shiny head.

Then I wake up.

18

3-18-2020:

- Stretch + Yoga: 5 min.
- Sit-Ups: Some
- Push-Ups: 100 (50/50)
- Chin-Ups: 45 (15/15/15)
- Leg Raises from bar: 30 (15/15)
- Standing Squats: 0
- Cardio: 30-min. walk

19

I haven't heard from Jesse, who lives with his mom and sister in Brooklyn, in several days. This morning, I texted him three times in a row, increasingly, irrationally frantic, to see if he is okay.

Finally, around four P.M., I hear from him: *Babe, babe, I'm okay just been sleeping—lol*

I text a smiling emoji with sunglasses, trying to play it cool.

"Thank God," I say to myself.

Young Couple in the Park
July 28, 2018

2 0

I live kitty-corner from a Mobil gas station, one of the very few gas stations left in Manhattan. For the past decade, I've heard so much honking, arguing, drunken yelling in the middle of the night, fist-fighting even, emanating from that tiny piece of New York real estate, home to four precious gas pumps. What's so interesting but bizarre right now, at 6:31 P.M. on a Friday—when there would normally be a long line of cars lined up to get gas before driving home—is how quiet it is.

2 1

It is so quiet:

You can hear a bird singing.
You can hear a baby crying.
You can hear a single voice rising up from Eighth Avenue.
You can hear a bus idling near Horatio.
You can hear a conversation under my window.
You can hear a guy at a gas pump talking on his
cellphone.
You can hear a kid on a scooter in the park.
You can hear a person with a walker walking, the walker
scraping the sidewalk.
You can hear a madman ranting and raving somewhere.
You can hear someone hammering something someplace
uptown.
You can hear delivery guys' bike bells.
You can hear someone whistling as he walks.
You can hear yourself crying by yourself.

And in the enforced solitude and silence, you can sometimes hear yourself replaying moments in your life, things said or not said, done or not done, love expressed or not expressed, all the gratitude you've ever received, all the gratitude you've ever felt.

2 2

It's only a matter of days before all businesses not deemed essential will be shut down indefinitely by the city. My local barbershop, King of Cutz, saw it coming, packed things up, and closed its doors early, as I discovered when I went by to get a last haircut from my longtime barber, Alex, today. I felt crestfallen seeing the lights off, the red-white-and-blue barbershop pole not swirling. I then went straight home and shaved my head in solidarity. I'll return, with what hair I've got regrown, when Alex, the "King," reopens someday.

One doesn't usually appreciate how places like this—though deemed "inessential"—are, in a certain light, essential to the life you lead. Getting a haircut and a beard trim is always a source of pleasure for me. But it's not just the grooming a barber can provide; it's the overheard conversations, the company, the stories.

Alex first started cutting my hair two weeks after I arrived in New York. At the time, I lived in an apartment further down in the Village, and Alex worked for someone else, at a barbershop on West Fourth Street. I still have a vivid sense memory of the first time he trimmed my beard and moustache: how his fingers, holding scissors, smelled vaguely of a mix of Dial soap and Parliament cigarettes. Alex, an immigrant from Russia, is straight, married, and happens to be strikingly handsome. The majority of his clients in the Village are gay, and he's cool with everyone. Not long after Alex began cutting my hair, I started taking Oliver there, too. Lulled by the low hum of the buzzers grazing his skull, Oliver would fall asleep almost immediately, silently, in the chair. Alex would gently work around him, never waking him until he had finished.

After years of hard work and saving, Alex was able to open his own shop in the West Village about two years ago; it is right around the corner from my apartment. There's often a wait for a cut and I don't mind; he's always got some trippy EDM playing. "I come for the haircut, but I stay for the music," I tell Alex half-kiddingly.

I once asked him who cuts his hair—whom he trusts enough to do it—and he let out a sorrowful sigh: "It's sad, bro. Sometimes I wish I could take my head off and cut my own hair."

I laughed so hard my smock fell off.

More recently, I got into a good-natured argument with Alex about my overuse of the word *beautiful* when it came to men—men I photograph, men I see on the street, men I had seen in his shop's seats next to me.

"Billy, you can't just go around saying every man you see is beautiful," Alex said.

"Not 'every,' I don't say every man is," I objected.

Alex, who's about thirty years younger than me, turned off his clippers, leaned against the counter, and faced me, the picture of patience. "Here's the thing: Women are 'beautiful.' Men are—well, a man might be 'cute,' but—"

"It's true, you are kind of cute, Alex."

He laughed, disarmed. "Thank you, but—"

"Yes? You were saying . . . ?"

"A woman is beautiful, and a man is . . . handsome. You can say a man is handsome."

I let this sink in, milking the moment.

"Alex, I think I can live with that," I finally responded.

"Okay, good." He turned the clippers back on and finished my haircut.

How We Live Now
March 30, 2020

2 3

I saw a young woman kneeling on an empty strip of grass arranging what looked from afar like magnolia petals, and I thought to myself, *I wonder if she's making art?* I approached, far enough away not to make her uncomfortable but close enough that she could hear my voice: "Hey, hi there, are you making an art piece?"

She looked up with a smile but shook her head. "I'm making a mandala."

"That's art," I said.

She shrugged and returned to her task. There was a slight breeze, which made arranging the petals on the grass without having them fly away a problem to solve. She pressed each one firmly into the grass and, by her touch alone, somehow made them stick.

"Do you mind if I come closer?" I called out.

"Not at all," said the young woman, "come over."

I stood maybe twelve feet away and watched her consider her materials: twigs and sprigs in different lengths and widths, leaves, and grasses. She made quick decisions, stripping twigs of branchlets; breaking some in two; putting the leaves aside; and separating out the dried grasses from the green ones.

She began making a pattern around the lavender-tipped magnolia petals, occasionally sitting back to assess her work, eyeing it with the unmistakable eye of an artist.

"It's beautiful," I murmured, "beautiful . . ."

She beamed a wholesome smile, as if agreeing with me—but quite modestly so. Her shiny, long brown braids fell over her shoulders. I introduced myself, as did she. Her name was Jen. I said aloud what I was thinking: "It's pure intuition—the way you're making the pattern—isn't it?"

"Yeah, mostly. I don't know why but I just like making them, I always have," she said.

It's because you're making a whole universe out of what would otherwise go underfoot, unnoticed, I thought—a different universe from the one we are currently inhabiting.

"Do you want to add something to it?" she asked me.

I felt honored.

I began scouring the ground. At first all my eyes could see were the geese turds everywhere. But the more I looked, the more I noticed other things: sticks and twigs like those she had selected. I found a good one and returned.

She sat back and I placed my stripped twig on the northern side of the mandala.

"Nice," she whispered.

I stepped back.

She began expertly weaving the dried grass into a wreath shape with great concentration, clearly something she had done before, her beringed fingers moving quickly. She placed one wreath down then made another, larger in size, and placed it around the first.

I thought of the sun and the moon. And of an eclipse.

She sat back on her heels again. Gazing at the completed mandala, she nodded decisively as if it had said something to her, and she was answering in return:

Yes, she seemed to be saying silently, *yes* . . .

A Mandala
April 4, 2020

2 4

When the city ordered all "nonessential" businesses to shut down on March 22, I would not have expected that to include city parks. We are still allowed to take walks, after all, to get exercise outdoors. But today I found the High Line closed at every entrance due to Covid-19. I felt disappointed at first, and then thought: *I'll bet all those plants, grasses, ferns, and trees up there will enjoy the time to themselves, grow as wild and unruly as they'd like, free of the scrutinizing gaze and trampling feet of human beings.*

2 5

Skateboarders, traveling in packs of five or six or more, each a good two or three yards apart, have taken over the empty streets in the late afternoon.

Lying on my couch, I put down my book and just listen.

I love the sounds they make—their wheels, their voices, their laughter: life, rumbling forward.

26

There's one restaurant in my neighborhood that I especially love and would hate to see disappear. I like it not only for the food—simply presented, perfectly made grilled meats and vegetables, soups and noodles—but also because it is small yet quiet enough that you can have a conversation without yelling to be heard by your tablemate. The owner/chef, Joe, had to lay off all of his waiters, hosts, dishwashers, and cooks with the shutdown, though he's still allowed to make food to go. He is now doing it on his own. I've ordered takeout a few times—hoping to help him survive—as have some other fans around here.

I went in the other night to pick up my order (with gloved hands), and after I'd paid—sliding my credit card down the bar toward him—he said, "How about a drink? You have a minute?" (He looked like he could use one.)

"Yeah, for sure," I said, "but are you permitted?"

He shrugged—no one else was in the restaurant—and reached (with gloved hands) for an unopened bottle of Pinot Grigio.

"Not technically. Let's just call it a drink between friends."

He poured two glasses and stepped back while I retrieved one for myself. We raised our glasses to one another.

"Here's to New York," I said.

"Here's to New York," Joe said.

We drank a glass and talked from either end of the bar.

Short-Order Cook at a Restaurant That's Still Delivering
April 19, 2020

27

Grabbing a drink at a bar is another thing we are learning all too quickly we had taken for granted all too often for far too long. My go-to place was a place just down the block, the Tavern on Jane. It's got everything you'd want in a neighborhood bar: amiable bartenders, big-screen TVs for watching games, good food, and every conceivable character.

The tavern is still open for takeout, but the last drinks were served with the city's total shutdown. I miss it—the camaraderie of fellow beer-drinkers, bullshitters, tall tale–tellers, including me. I have collected so many stories about nights at "The Jane"—some of which I would not repeat—but one in particular has been making me smile recently:

I'm having a beer at the bar a few years back when a guy about my age two stools down looks up from the cellphone into which he's been gazing and says to no one in particular, "This ever happen to you?"

No one else in the vicinity seems to have noticed or heard him, so I reply, "What's that?"

"This is so messed up." He wipes a hand over his face, shakes his head, collects his thoughts, and continues: "So, a few days ago, I'm looking in my closet for something and I find this leather jacket—"

"Yeah . . . ?"

"It's not mine. It's not my jacket. It's not even a man's jacket. It's a woman's leather jacket, and I have no idea how it got there—"

I am already hooked.

"—Or how long it's been there. So I start to go through in my head whose it might be—you know, what women have I been seeing—she might have left it at my place by accident?"

"Right, right, I get it," I say.

"And I even ask this friend of mine who helps me shop—I'm really color-blind, and she buys shit for me, shirts and pants and stuff that match in a way I could never see, and so I ask her, 'Did you see that leather jacket in my closet?' And she says, 'Yeah, it's been there for at least two months.'"

"*Two months?*" I interject.

"Yeah, I know—two months! But at least that helps me narrow it down. So I figure it's gotta be one of either two women. That's my theory. I text one and ask her if she maybe left her leather jacket. Haven't heard back from her—not surprised, really; that one didn't end well. And then the other woman, I just texted her, and she texted right back, but kind of snotty—like, '*Oh, you can't even keep track of all the women in your bed?*'"

The guy pauses, thinking this through, and adds, "I mean, she added a smiley face, so I don't think she was too pissed off. But anyway—"

"—It wasn't her jacket either," I fill in.

"*Exactly*, it wasn't her jacket. And I don't know who the fuck's it is."

"Okay, hold on, let's pause for a second," I say, "first, let me compliment you on at least *trying* to return the jacket. Most guys would just toss it or whatever. I left a blue sweater at a guy's apartment a couple weeks ago, and I still haven't gotten it back . . ."

The bartender, Lily, has only been half-listening but has gotten the entire gist of the story. "So, Tom—" evidently, his name is Tom "—you should make it a Cinderella story—now you set out to find a girl who fits *into* the leather jacket."

"And then what? I'm no Prince Charming," he says with a snort.

Lily smiles. "Never know," she says.

"I was thinking of selling it, actually," he tells me sotto voce. "Hey, Lily! Lily! Here, take a look—" he finds a picture of the jacket on his phone, zooms in on it, shows it to her, "twenty-five dollars, I'll give it to you for twenty-five dollars."

She laughs and walks away to make someone a drink.

"Let me see," I say, and the guy—Tom—hands me his phone. The picture shows a mid-length black leather jacket with lots of zippers, hanging forlornly from a hanger, half on, half off, in an otherwise pretty bare closet.

I hand the phone back to him with a chuckle.

"It took you *two months* before you realized it was there? I'm sorry, but that part is hilarious."

He shrugs like, *What can I say?*

"Women," he mutters.

"Men," I mutter in return.

There's a long pause, and then I tell him I want to buy him a drink.

Tom looks back at me like he doesn't understand what I have just said. I've found there are few things more unnerving to certain straight men—not all, but some—than a gay guy buying them a drink.

"*Can* I buy you a drink?" I say, putting it more directly. "May I?"

"A drink? Um, sure, why not," though he doesn't look at all sure this is a good idea.

Lily pours him a glass of wine, and refills mine.

"Cheers," I say, "thank you for that story."

Tom and I clink glasses.

"You're welcome," he says.

NY, NY, NY—Times Square
September 1, 2017

2 8

Liquor stores—unquestionably "essential"—are still open around here. Here's how it currently works at the place in my neighborhood: Only five customers in the store at a time; social distancing required; and so forth. They deliver, too, but I wanted to go in and see how the men of Manley's Wine & Spirits were doing the other day. It was empty.

Begloved, I placed my bottle of wine on the counter and Omar, who knows me all too well, scanned it with a handheld scanner. I swiped my card in the machine. When it came to signing my name with the little wand, Omar said, "I think I know you well enough to sign for you—is that okay?"

"I'm sure you do, go for it."

With a few quick strokes, he did, then showed me his forgery: in place of my name, he'd drawn two little dots for eyes and a squiggly smile line underneath, like a child's drawing of a face.

"That's how you sign it, right?" Omar said.

"That is exactly how. Thank you, my friend, and take care."

2 9

One might think that being sequestered for weeks, being unable to go to a gym or swim, and being just plain bored would translate into even more motivation to exercise at home.

I am finding this is not the case.

I look at the simple chart I made to keep track of my home exercise routine—columns for stretching, yoga, sit-ups, cardio, etc.—certain that I would be doing 150 push-ups a day within a week.

All the chart's columns are empty over the past nine days.

Conversely, however, I am spending far more time than usual in the kitchen, cooking. Since Oliver died, I'd lived as he had lived before meeting me: never cooking at home, getting takeout or buying premade things, like a roast chicken and sides, at the deli or—my version of his eating sardines over the sink—eating cereal for dinner. I'd found cooking for one—me—depressing.

But now, with so much time on my hands, I am shopping more attentively (making grocery lists—imagine that), tracking down recipes, and making dinners for myself while listening to music on WQXR, our classical music station. It feels good—good to be away from screens (computer and phone and TV), good to be creating something (even when things don't work out well), good to be reviving my once-respectable cooking skills, good for my well-being. I set a place at the table—placemat, napkin, silverware—turn up the music, and have a meal with myself. Tonight: salty roasted cashews and almonds to nibble on; simply sautéed salmon, green beans, and brown rice with scallions. And a bowl of strawberry ice cream.

Manhattan Beauty
April 14, 2020

3 0

A letter arrives via email:

Dear Mr. Hayes,

A few years ago, I was at the bar at the Corner Bistro on Jane Street, presumably near your house. My friend told me that he was reading *The Mind's Eye* by Oliver Sacks, and I started talking about how Dr. Sacks had to be the strangest, most interesting man, as he is self-diagnosed with so many neurological conditions (face-blindness, etc.) and has so many eclectic interests. Literally a few minutes later, Dr. Sacks, wearing plaid on plaid, came in, pulled up a stool, and sat between us smiling. I was in shock and speechless, but he looked at me as if he knew me. After a few seconds, you came by and said something to him (maybe to tell him that he didn't know us or we weren't you?) and led him to a table in the back. It's been among my greatest regrets that I was too flummoxed to say hello.

So, if I may, belatedly: "Hello, Dr. Sacks."

P.S., I am now a neuroscientist at Yale.

Best wishes, _____

3 1

A text from Jesse:

"Hey"

"Hey"

"I feel like I'm losing you."

"No. Not lost. I'm here," I say.

We decide to meet at the Christopher Street Pier. We're not breaking any rules—people are allowed to take walks, to exercise, to meet in public, as long as social distancing is practiced.

I wait and wait. Finally, I see him shuffling down the block in his hoodie and an overcoat—it's really chilly and windy out. He looks adorable.

Reflexively, he leans down to hug me—he towers a good six inches above me—and I want to, too—I want to warm him up—but I gently push him away—"No, no, no, no hugging, remember, no kissing, not yet." Which makes me feel at once guilty, sad, cruel, sensible, stupid, old—thirty-three years older than he is.

He steps back with a smile, and we walk to the end of the pier and have a pretty good chat. But it's awkward, unnatural: to want something—someone—so near to you, you could have it if you really wanted it, but you can't, you won't, you don't. And you don't know if you will ever have a chance again.

3 2

On my way back home, I spotted three young men exercising vigorously—I mean, *really* vigorously—on the otherwise deserted pier. I noticed Army insignias on their shorts and shirts and couldn't resist calling out, "You guys are in the military?"

They came a little closer to me as I stood on one of the cement risers, at least twenty feet between us.

"Yeah, we are," one said.

"Huh, my dad was too—a Korean War vet," I said. "He went to West Point, class of 1949."

Their eyes widened a bit at that ancient date.

"We're at West Point," one replied.

"No way! You guys are all at West Point? What are you, uh, what are you guys doing here in the city?"

"We're medics," said one more soberly, "and he's an RN," gesturing to the fellow to his left. "We came down for training for, well, for—"

"—for the crisis?" I said, completing his thought.

I couldn't get the word "pandemic" out of my mouth.

He nodded. "Yeah. We're headed back up to West Point this afternoon to work in the clinic there for any soldiers who—you know—"

By now, I was blinking back tears: "For soldiers or cadets who get sick . . . ?"

All three nodded.

I thought about my late father and how proud he'd be of them.

"Thank you, thank you for what you're doing."

We all introduced ourselves before I asked, "May I take your picture?"

"Sure," the three soldiers said.

I took a few of the group, then a couple of each solo.

One of them—Shane was his name—asked if I would send him the pictures.

"Sure, of course, how about I give you my number, then text me and I'll send them on to you. Okay?"

I called out my phone number across the green field.

I asked Shane to read it back to me—just to be sure he got it right.

I haven't heard from him since. I wonder what's happened with him.

West Point Medics Exercising at the Pier
March 30, 2020

3 3

Headline in the *New York Times*, March 31: IT'S TIME TO MAKE YOUR OWN FACE MASK

The situation has changed yet again.

Days earlier, we were told that masks are necessary only for frontline workers, and they should not be used—and certainly not hoarded—by those who don't need them.

But okay, I get it, I understand how contagious this virus is. I read about the latest science emerging from virologists, epidemiologists, public health officials, and there seems to be a consensus that masks may help. At this point, they are recommended but not required. Only problem is, you can't buy a protective face mask anywhere, or order one online to get here any time soon. I see handmade signs taped to phone poles advertising N95 masks for sale, $10 apiece, with a phone number on tear-off strips at the bottom—all but two are taken. It could very well be a scam.

I search my apartment, but I do not have a bandana or a scarf like those shown in DIY videos. I try making a mask out of a vacuum cleaner bag, cutting it apart and using shoelaces for ties—someone suggested this somewhere on social media—but when I look in the mirror, I scare myself. I look like a cartoon of a cartoon of a terrorist. I also can't breathe. I end up making a makeshift mask out of a pair of Calvin Klein briefs; it'll do.

3 4

I walk east on Fourteenth Street and toward Union Square. Aside from a few scattered people scurrying by with multiple bags of groceries, the only people I see for long stretches are homeless people.

The still-wintry wind has a mean bite to it.

I can't wait for summer.

I see Raheem's shopping carts before I spot him—five of them, lined up near the curb, each overflowing with the recyclable bottles and cans he collects for money to live on. Raheem, whom I've known for more than five years, is wearing a winter coat and hat and is huddled under blankets in a doorway on the sidewalk. Raheem's name means "merciful" in Arabic, he told me when we first met. I'll never forget that.

We talk for a while. Raheem knows how to protect himself in this pandemic. He has gloves and wipes and hand sanitizer tucked under the blankets, as he shows me. Raheem would never sleep in a homeless shelter even during the best of times—he stopped trying those years ago—and he's heard they're "death traps" these days.

I ask how he's getting along.

"Getting along," he echoes softly in reply, "getting along."
I give him a twenty, as I always do, before going on my way.

"Peace and hallelujah," Raheem says.

"Peace and hallelujah," I say in return.

Raheem on Fourteenth Street
March 31, 2020

35

I don't have a car or drive in New York, so this thought hadn't occurred to me: Yesterday, I spoke to a friend in Washington state who's hunkered down in her small house together with her family of three plus the boyfriend of her grown daughter, and she is trying to work remotely. When cabin fever hits, she gets in her car and drives. And drives. And drives. On the nearly empty roadways and freeways in Seattle. Music blasting: Whitney Houston, Mariah Carey, Michael Jackson.

When she told me this, my first thought was: What a great idea for a film: a working mom who can't take it anymore, grabs a bottle of hand sanitizer and a couple rolls of toilet paper, gets in her car and flees—drives cross-country, coast to coast and back again by different routes, sleeping in her car and squatting in abandoned buildings, until the whole damn pandemic is over.

3 6

The president may say and make up what he wants to hear about how well he's handling things, but one thing cannot be denied: Deaths are hard to hide. By April 1, far more Americans have already been killed by the coronavirus (more than five thousand) than by the September 11 attacks. In New York City alone, more than one thousand people have perished in the past thirty days. That figure reminds me of Larry Kramer's prophetic early AIDS essay "1,112 and Counting," published in the *New York Native* in March 1983—yet that number referred to *cases*, not deaths. Now, thirty-seven years later, thirty-two million people around the world have died of AIDS, according to the World Health Organization. What will the toll be ultimately from Covid-19?

3 7

I took a bunch of photos today, but more of *things*—signs, flowers, scaffolding—than of people. People are becoming scarcer on the streets—and they look scared and unapproachable. But then on West Fourth Street, I came upon three young men (late twenties, I'd guess) sitting on a stoop having drinks and takeout, chatting, around six P.M.

It was such an unlikely sight—people sitting on their stoop! Like something from a different time—summertime, perhaps—or a daydream.

From a proper distance, I stopped and said hello, showed them my camera, and asked if I could take a picture. They all said, "Sure." I told them what I was up to, trying to take street photos during the pandemic, and almost in unison they said, "We all had it, we all had Covid."

"What? You guys had it?" I probably unconsciously took a step back or two—or more.

One of the three explained that they are residents in anesthesiology at NYU Medical Center, where Covid swept through in

February—before it became clear this was a global pandemic. They thought it was just a flu bug at first.

"At least half the people in our entire program got it, maybe more." Everyone had recovered, including the three of them, without any special treatment, just rest. "It sucked," one said, and they all agreed that it "sucked for sure," saying it was like having a bad flu—two days of high fever and chills, and then four or five days before they felt better. They laughed as one chimed in, saying, "I've been way, way sicker and still had to show up for classes or at the hospital." And indeed, the three young men, sitting on a stoop eating delivered Mexican food, looked the picture of health.

One of the three told me that they'd already been tested for antibodies to the coronavirus and they all were found to have antibodies to it (as had their colleagues), which may mean they are now immune. They have since given their plasma for further study, and they have been back at work for weeks. We chatted for a while longer. I thanked them for what they are doing and for letting me take their picture, and I headed home.

Doctors from NYU
April 2, 2020

3 8

Because I've worked at home for years now, the mandate to stay home and work from home is, I imagine, a little easier for someone like me. I'm also a loner and an introvert (except when it comes to strangers), which helps too.

Even so, there are times when I feel spooked—not scared but spooked. I wish Jesse were here to get under the covers with.

Making things worse, the wind has been howling all day and night like an overdone sound effect in a horror movie—one that goes on for ten or twelve hours, not two. I turn on WQXR to drown it out—all three Bose radios tuned to the same station but in different rooms: one in the kitchen, one in my office, one in the bedroom. My entire apartment is filled with beautiful noise. Oliver used to love to do this at night—turn on all the radios at once; hearing Bach was his favorite—and just soak up the music, as if in a bath at the perfect temperature, 110 degrees.

Tonight, as I pace and worry, I am stopped in my tracks by a Clara Schumann composition: *Three Romances*, opus 11, it's called, I later find out. I hadn't known it. I stand somewhere in the middle among all the radios, eyes closed. The stark piano music acts like a ghostbuster, ridding my apartment of all howling spooks.

I look out the window: there's just emptiness—nothingness. I almost expect to see tumbleweeds blowing down Eighth Avenue.

Clara Schumann's music swells.

3 9

It is a spring evening in the Village about four years ago:

I stop by the smoke shop down the block. It's six o'clock. Ali has arrived for work just as Bobby is finishing his shift. I've hardly ever seen them here together; it's either one or the other behind the counter. They are talking about something with great vigor and animation—at least, that's how it appears to me. I can't understand a word they're saying.

"Gentlemen. *Gentlemen?*" I can hardly get their attention, they're so enthralled. Finally, I have to interrupt: "Hey, what are you two arguing about? And, which language are you speaking?"

"Panjabi," says Ali, ignoring my first question. Bobby has walked away, into the back somewhere. Ali calls after him, as if getting in a final jab. He can't disguise his delight. He is a cat waiting for the mouse to return to play.

Moments pass. Bobby is back at the counter, as if nothing had happened between them, and I have to smile: Here they are, side by side, these two from whom I've been buying Sunday papers and rolling papers, bottles of water and Kit Kat bars and poppers for the past seven years: one Muslim man, one Hindu, matching mischievous grins on their light-brown faces.

"Yes?" says Ali.

"Mr. Billy, what can we do for you?" says Bobby, feigning seriousness.

Now I can't even remember what I came in here for, so I change course.

"Teach me a word in Panjabi," I say. "Just one word."

"Okay," says Ali.

"All right," says Bobby.

They stare back at me, waiting for a prompt.

"Hold on, let me think. What is—um, what is the Panjabi word for *beauty*?"

They look at one another.

"*Sohni*," says Bobby.

Ali nods, "Yes, *sohni*," then adds, "but it's *sohna* if you're talking about a man—*sohna*, not *sohni*."

Ali: he knows me all too well.

"That is very helpful—thank you, Ali," I say.

"You're welcome, my friend."

Anzar
April 2, 2020

4 0

On the day Oliver died, Ali was the first person to whom I told the news. He had gotten to know "The Doctor" well over the years, and they shared a mutual affection and respect. I remember how Ali came out from behind the counter to comfort me: "I will pray for the Doctor," he said tenderly, "and for you."

He's been a constant in my life since, almost like a family member, despite the obvious differences between us, as he is a devout Muslim, Pakistani American, not to mention a husband, a father, and a vegetarian teetotaler—and I am, well, I am none of those things. I can't walk past the smoke shop without at least waving or saying hello to Ali, if not stopping in to chat. And if I don't, Ali spots me on his sidewalk surveillance cameras—and gives me shit about it the next time I come in.

Now, though, I haven't seen Ali at the shop in about three weeks, and I'm beginning to seriously worry. The only times I've known him to be away for so long (besides his one day off a week) were when he'd gone back to Pakistan to see family—visits he made once every couple of years.

I've popped my head into the shop several times and asked whomever was behind the counter—men I did not recognize— about Ali: "Is he okay?"

Yes, they always said, he's okay, but nothing more. Maybe they didn't know? Maybe they didn't want to say?

The other night, I saw the owner of the smoke shop standing out front, wearing an N95 mask. We'd met a few times before. I approached and said hello, while keeping a proper distance.

"How's Ali? I haven't seen him in so long. He's not sick, is he?"

"Yes, Ali's sick, unfortunately," the owner said.

No. Fuck.

I called Ali's number the minute I got home but it went to voicemail. My heart sank. But he called me back a short time later. I was relieved and happy to hear his voice and told him that. "I hear you've been sick. Tell me—where are you, how are you doing?"

"I'm home. Yes, ill," he said, "very, very bad." It had started two weeks ago—high fever, coughing, weak, impossible to eat. "I felt like I'm done," Ali said. *"Done."*

Beyond the words he spoke, I could hear the fear in his voice. Without having to ask, I knew that his fear was more for his wife and two children—both now college students—than for himself.

"The fever would not go away," he continued, "it was not easy, not easy, very painful, but then, the doctor gave me some pills— antibiotics." He said he'd been able to talk to the doctor via "telemedicine," a term that, at an earlier time, I would never have expected to hear from Ali. Or from me, for that matter.

"And the pills worked?"

At this, Ali sounded happy for the first time. "Oh yes, the fever went away. The cough, too. Thank God. Everything's good now, thank God—"

"Yes, thank God, and your family—your wife, your kids?"

"Everyone's okay, everyone's safe, healthy. Thank God, thank God." He sounded tired. Very tired.

I told him I'd keep him in my thoughts and check back in.

We wished each other a good night.

4 1

It's a little like losing your life while still being alive, this experience. Everything I knew in New York—everything *we* knew—is gone: stores, restaurants, concerts, subway rides, church services, movie theaters, museums, nail salons. When a memory comes, you almost wonder if it is true—it seems so impossible to imagine again—if it happened at all:

A very tall man, six-four or more—my age at least; handsome face—stands on a subway platform with a very small girl (four, maybe five years old). She is immaculately dressed, all in bright greens and pinks, and her hair is a garden of blooms, each fixed with a light pink ribbon.

His skin is the color and sheen of coffee beans; hers is caramel with lots of cream. She holds his hand; it must be her grandfather, I think to myself. The subway is delayed. He distracts her by dancing, taking both her hands in his and dancing; music in his head. She giggles. When he lets go of her hands, she keeps dancing on her own and now he laughs; a little girl dancing freely on the subway plat-form, so sweet but also fascinating: You can see how rhythm is built into the body.

A subway arrives, and he ushers her on, holding her cat's-sized hand in his giant paw. They sit across from me; the tiny girl is pinioned safely between the big man's knees.

"She is adorable," I can't help saying, "and her hair—did you do that for her?"

He nods, like it's no big deal. "Had to learn how. I have six daughters. Viv's my youngest."

The man smiles, a touch rueful. The little girl looks up at her dad. He opens a small bottle of water and holds it to her mouth. She takes a sip.

4 2

Nighttime: I hear salsa music on a car radio across the street. And nothing else. Just the salsa music.

We could be in Spokane on a summer night.

That's how quiet it is in Manhattan.

In the silence, the first place my mind goes is back in time a few years.

It's late, a Friday night, eleven or so:

Exiting the elevator in my building, I see my next-door neighbor pacing the lobby, radiating, as he often does, the nervous energy of someone dying for a smoke (Alex is perpetually trying to quit). But he isn't the only jumpy one. Our unflappable doorman, Vinnie, seems on edge too.

"What's going on?" I say.

"There's a naked man with a cape standing outside," Alex booms.

He has a voice that booms.

Surely, I'd misheard, like Oliver, whose mishearings throughout the day, every day, could make life surreal.

"Yep," confirms Vinnie, standing watch at the door.

I peek outside, but what I see isn't at all what you might expect on hearing there's a naked man with a cape—a Halloween costume, say, or lack thereof. No, he is a tall man on the opposite corner, entirely naked but for something raggedy around his neck. Alex and I step outside. The streets are jammed with cars and cabs.

"He must be super high—"

I nod, adding it all up.

"I'm getting shorts," Alex adds.

This doesn't compute; Alex is already wearing shorts. Now he is talking on his phone: "Yeah, anything—those old Gap shorts—and a T-shirt!" he booms; he is talking to his wife, up in their apartment.

Just then, the naked man begins crossing the street against the traffic, coming toward us, as if magnetized.

Alex lights a cigarette, the picture of unfazed. He must have seen such things on numerous occasions, it strikes me—he's a restaurant owner and lives his life at night, mostly on the East Side. But, on the contrary: "This is something I have never seen in all my years in New York," he volunteers.

"Me either," murmurs Vinnie.

As we watch, Alex mentions that he'll be selling his apartment and moving soon—probably out of Manhattan. "This is the kind of shit I'll miss, though."

He takes a long drag.

The naked man has almost reached us when Alex's wife appears, but then the guy turns and begins walking the other way. Alex grabs the clothes, and the two of us catch up with him.

"Hey man, put these on," Alex says, as emphatically as a bouncer throwing someone out of a club, "you don't want trouble with cops, you don't want to get arrested."

He takes them but his eyes are uncomprehending. It is only then I notice the cape is a hospital gown. He must have walked out of an ER or a psychiatric ward. We watch him stumble up Eighth Avenue, holding the shorts but not stopping to put them on.

"You tried, dude," I say to Alex, "that was very cool of you."

He shrugs: "I don't give a shit if he's naked, or high, but the guy's out of his mind. Anyway, I already called 911—he needs to be back in a hospital before he gets hit by a car or put in jail."

He takes his wife's hand, they walk off in the other direction, and, as sirens begin to blare, I think to myself: *That's what neighborliness is*: You care enough to make sure there's no trouble, but not so much that you get completely embroiled in others' lives and problems. This city is so dense, so intense, so compressed, so stressed, so dirty, so diverse, so tough on the outside, so transparent in how it wears its heart on its sleeve, that you cannot survive here without occasional help from strangers.

UPS Deliverymen
April 14, 2020

4 3

A story from my friend Kate:

"Yesterday I was riding my bike home to Williamsburg from my job in Long Island City when I was stopped at a red light next to a car, and the man driving must have seen me wipe my nose on my sleeve (simply from the cold weather) so he stuck out a handful of tissues and said 'Do you need a tissue? They're clean!'

"Pre-Covid I would've taken it but now I'm so paranoid to touch anything! I smiled and said no thanks, but then he stuck his other arm holding the tissue box out the window:

"'You sure?'

"I laughed and said 'Yes, I'm ok, but thank you so much.'

"'All right, stay safe, baby,' he said, and he drove off.

"Such a New York moment; makes me miss these unexpected interactions and kind gestures. I think we're all going to suffer from a sort of PTSD, I guess I'm kind of feeling it already. In the end we're all connected through this, and I must say I'm pretty proud of the awareness and caution (most) everyone in NYC is displaying."

4 4

I got a call on Sunday at 1:20 P.M. from a number I did not recognize, so I didn't answer. It was a 215 number with no caller ID.

I suppose I was feeling lonely here in my place by myself because then I thought, *Maybe it's a friend—someone with a new number?*

I decided to text it: "Who's this? No name comes up," I wrote.

"Mrs. M." came the answer right away. That's all the text said.

Mrs. M . . . I don't know any *Mrs. Ms,* do I? I couldn't think of one, so I paid it no mind.

But then the same number, a Philadelphia number, called again and left a voicemail on Tuesday.

I hate listening to voicemails for some reason. Preoccupied by work, I waited until today to read the iPhone transcription (as bad as they often are).

It read:

"Hello this is Susan M_____ calling I just calling to check in with you um got a text message for me earlier and I'm just wanting to know how things are going for you during this time feel free to give me a call or text me back all right talk to you soon I hope you're doing well thank you so much bye-bye"

Well, I thought to myself, I do not know who this "Susan" is, but that is a very nice message. So I called the number back. The person picked up after one ring.

"Hi, my name is Bill. You called me? And, uh, are you sure you have the right number? I saw your text. 'Mrs. M'?"

"Oh. You're not ____," she said, "the parent of _____ ?"

"No."

"No?"

"No. Definitely no children here."

Pause.

"I live in New York," I added. "Who are you trying to reach?"

Mrs. M. went silent again, then said: "I'm a special ed teacher at ____, and I'm trying to make sure all the students are set up before we start, before we start remote learning—technology and stuff—"

"Well you sound very nice, and like you're a great teacher, but, um, you have the wrong number—"

We compared numbers—she *did* have mine, but must have missed a number, or taken it down incorrectly. "Oh . . ." She sounded concerned, unsure what to do.

We chatted awhile. I asked how she was doing (fine). She asked how I was doing (fine). I told her I'm a writer and a photographer.

"Well, now that you have my number, call me if you ever need a resource to talk about teachers. Trying to teach special ed remotely— it's, it's—

"It must be really hard," I said.

She put it differently: "It's a challenge . . ."

I told her it was a pleasure to meet her, to connect with a kind stranger even in such a random way, and I wished her well. She wished me well too.

I said goodbye to Mrs. M.

Chelsea Boys
April 19, 2020

Security Patrol Officers, Chelsea Housing Complex
April 19, 2020

4 5

I came upon a couple of firemen today who were taking a break outside their truck. I asked if I could take their picture, but they said no. We talked for a while. "So are things slower since the city's so quiet?" I asked.

One of the two shook his head. "There are still fires and heart attacks," he said.

46

I have a few friends, some of whom I've photographed, who are escorts: hookers, rent men, go-go boys, or masseurs who make outcalls on the side. Two or three are able to charge $300 an hour and $2,000 plus expenses for a weekend-long "Boyfriend Experience" (minimum two orgasms a day), making as much as $100K a year on their bodies and smiles and personalities alone. But now? The pandemic has put them out to pasture. Perhaps permanently.

But the johns still call.

"My clients have sent me messages begging me to come over, pay me double, triple, whatever I want!" my friend Scott, aka Chloe, texts me. Sure, they could do Zoom sex or old-fashioned phone sex, he adds, but not at the same rates and it's just not the same anyway: "Everyone is dying for touch and human contact."

Tell me about it.

"You can't kiss a computer screen," I text back.

4 7

We've had eight hundred people die each day for several days in a row in New York, most of them here in the city, and most of these among communities of color in the Bronx and Queens. Eight hundred. It's hard for me—for any of us—to fully comprehend those numbers. Some of the unclaimed dead are being buried in mass graves on Hart Island, just off the coast of the Bronx, which sounds beyond ghastly, though I do understand the necessity. Even so, I can't help wondering why they don't cremate these bodies—that would seem far more dignified than tossing them into burial pits.

Nor can I imagine how painful it must be for families, spouses, children, who can't even be at the bedside to hold a hand and say goodbye and kiss a forehead (visitors are not allowed in hospitals). And even more, how frightening it must be for those patients, quarantined in ICUs, on ventilators, dying with no loved ones around, no familiar faces. I just read about a young doctor who'd had to facilitate three "farewells" in one day from families via FaceTime for her dying patients. I suppose it is better than nothing, and we should be grateful that such technology even exists.

At the same time, I think about how gentle Oliver's death was by comparison, how gentle a death *can* be. Oliver died at home in his own bed, as he had wished, with me and his longtime friend, Kate, on either side of him. A hospice nurse stood by to guide and advise us through the final stages. After he'd passed, we were able to stay with him until the undertakers arrived to take him to the funeral home. From what I am told, most victims of Covid-related deaths are denied those comforts and those rituals—as are their families— across nearly every part of the globe.

Making Peace with the Hudson
April 4, 2020

4 8

9:25 P.M. Three police officers patrolling on horseback ride up a silenced Eighth Avenue, unimpeded by cars, traffic, people; there's something so comforting in the *clop, clop, clop* of the horses' hooves through my open windows.

At the same time, I think of a funeral cortege.

4 9

It is four winters ago, and I am standing at a streetlight on Greenwich
Avenue:

I hear a young couple right next to me talking about a large
apartment building opposite, a prewar brownstone probably twenty-
five stories high. They are gazing skyward, smiling and in awe: "Oh,
look at those windows! And the ceilings!"

"Wouldn't it be great to live there," I say to them.

The light changes green.

"It would!" they say in unison as we set out.

"Let's," I add, "let's live there."

"Okay," says the boy.

"Yeah, definitely," says the girl.

"We'll just get, like, thirty people, cool people like us to go in on
it, and then we'll be able to live there," the boy adds, as if just clari-
fying the arrangements.

"I'm in," I say. "You?"

"Definitely."

"But only the best place in the building," I add.

"The one with turrets," she says.

We've come to the other corner. I point to myself: "Billy, I'm Billy."

"Rachel," says the girl.

"Adam," says the boy. "We'll be in touch, Billy, we'll be in touch."

We never get around to exchanging numbers. They go to the left; I keep going straight.

"Good night," I call to them over my shoulder.

5 0

When you look out and see the empty streets and sidewalks and shuttered shops, a friend tells me, see it as *solidarity*—everyone doing their best to keep themselves and everyone else healthy.

I try to remember this, remind myself of this, repeat this to myself, as I walk around my neighborhood: *solidarity, solidarity.* Even so, I can't deny how sad and disorienting the absence of life in these once-busy streets seems.

And then I meet a kind fellow: a pharmacist at a small independent shop on Fourteenth Street. He is providing two free disposable face masks to anyone, no questions asked or purchase required, whether you're a customer or a homeless person. (There's a big sign on his shop window.) I don't have one myself—you can't buy any at any franchise drugstores and our government sure isn't handing them out; I've been using masks made from underwear or cloth napkins—so I knocked on the locked door. The pharmacist came at once to open it and, when I asked about masks, gave me two enclosed in a sealed sanitary bag. I was grateful to receive them and said so. I never did catch the pharmacist's name, I'm afraid. I offered him a tip. He refused it.

A Pharmacist on Fourteenth Street
April 9, 2020

5 1

57 Days in the Pandemic in the United States of America:

Thurs. May 7: 1,292,623 confirmed cases & 76,928 dead*
Weds. May 6: 1,263,183 confirmed cases & 74,807 dead
Tues. May 5: 1,237,633 confirmed cases & 72,271 dead
Mon. May 4: 1,212,900 confirmed cases & 69,921 dead
Sun. May 3: 1,188,122 confirmed cases & 68,598 dead
Sat. May 2: 1,160,774 confirmed cases & 67,444 dead
Fri. May 1: 1,131,492 confirmed cases & 65,776 dead
Thurs. April 30: 1,095,304 confirmed cases & 63,871 dead
Weds. April 29: 1,064,533 confirmed cases & 61,668 dead
Tues. April 28: 1,035,765 confirmed cases & 59,266 dead
Mon. April 27: 1,008,043 confirmed cases & 56,649 dead
Sun. April 26: 987,322 confirmed cases & 55,415 dead
Sat. April 25: 960,896 confirmed cases & 54,265 dead
Fri. April 24: 925,038 confirmed cases & 52,185 dead
Thurs. April 23: 880,204 confirmed cases & 49,845 dead
Weds. April 22: 848,994 confirmed cases & 47,676 dead
Tues. April 21: 824,147 confirmed cases & 45,318 dead

Mon. April 20: 792,759 confirmed cases & 42,514 dead

Sun. April 19: 764,177 confirmed cases & 40,665 dead

Sat. April 18: 735,086 confirmed cases & 38,910 dead

Fri. April 17: 700,282 confirmed cases & 36,997 dead

Thurs. April 16: 671,425 confirmed cases & 33,286 dead

Wed. April 15: 638,111 confirmed cases & 30,844 dead

Tues. April 14: 609,240 confirmed cases & 26,033 dead

Mon. April 13: 581,918 confirmed cases & 23,608 dead

Sun. April 12: 556,044 confirmed cases & 22,073 dead

Sat. April 11: 527,111 confirmed cases & 20,506 dead

Fri. April 10: 501,560 confirmed cases & 18,777 dead

Thurs. April 9: 462,385 confirmed cases & 16,595 dead

Weds. April 8: 432,132 confirmed cases & 14,817 dead

Tues. April 7: 398,185 confirmed cases & 12,844 dead

Mon. April 6: 368,079 confirmed cases & 10,923 dead

Sun. April 5: 337,072 confirmed cases & 9,619 dead

Sat. April 4: 312,237 confirmed cases & 8,502 dead

Fri. April 3: 277,953 confirmed cases & 7,152 dead

Thurs. April 2: 245,070 confirmed cases & 5,949 dead

Weds. April 1: 215,417 confirmed cases & 5,116 dead

Tues. March 31: 188,172 confirmed cases & 3,873 dead

Mon. March 30: 160,020 confirmed cases & 2,953 dead

Sun. March 29: 140,886 confirmed cases & 2,467 dead

Sat. March 28: 122,666 confirmed cases & 2,147 dead

Fri. March 27: 103,942 confirmed cases & 1,689 dead

Thurs. March 26: 83,507 confirmed cases & 1,201 dead

Weds. March 25: 69,197 confirmed cases & 1,050 dead

Tues. March 24: 51,542 confirmed cases & 674 dead

Mon. March 23: 46,332 confirmed cases & 610 dead

Sun. March 22: 33,276 confirmed cases & 417 dead
Sat. March 21: 26,138 confirmed cases & 323 dead
Fri. March 20: 19,352 confirmed cases & 260 dead
Thurs. March 19: 13,680 confirmed cases & 200 dead
Weds. March 18: 8,017 confirmed cases & 143 dead
Tues. March 17: 6,362 confirmed cases & 108 dead
Mon. March 16: 4,427 confirmed cases & 86 dead
Sun. March 15: 3,486 confirmed cases & 66 dead
Sat. March 14: 2,695 confirmed cases & 58 dead
Fri. March 13: 2,100 confirmed cases & 48 dead
Thurs. March 12: 1,663 confirmed cases & 40 dead

* More than one third of these deaths were in New York

(Sources: Johns Hopkins Covid-19 Dashboard and
www.worldometers.info/coronavirus/)

Doorman Near Thirty-fourth Street
April 14, 2020

5 2

One of the few positive things to come out of this crisis is that many of us are renewing friendships we've let go by the wayside (inadvertently usually), in part because we now have more time on our hands, but also because we are more aware than ever of how poignantly short life can be. Over the past five or six weeks, I've caught up by text, phone, Zoom, or FaceTime chats with many friends I hadn't talked to or seen in years. That includes a few friends-with-benefits like my old buddy Mark. Mark and I began exchanging texts on Instagram one night in late March. It was flirty at first. We were both horny, sequestered solo, and exchanged a few shameless selfies. (I had no idea he had such an extensive wardrobe of sexy underwear.) We hadn't been in touch or seen each other in at least a year, maybe a year and a half, even though he lives in the city, albeit six or seven miles north. Mark makes great music playlists and he sent a few along with his pictures—"Pandemic Playlists," as he called them, with the old school R&B we both love.

When I didn't hear back from him after a few days, I didn't think about it. A couple nights ago, I checked in.

"How's it going," I texted casually.

"Unfortunately, the virus got me. Started feeling symptoms on Saturday, connected with my doctor on Monday, and have been in strict self-quarantine since then"

"My God how do u feel?"

"Tuesday and Wednesday were bad. I've had a fever of 102.3 consistently. . . . chills, body aches, headache, fatigue, loss of smell and taste, and then most recently, nausea/vomiting—"

"—Shit, *everything*—I am so sorry—"

"—and a sore throat too—lol"

A row of three red rose emojis was all I could come up with as a reply.

I felt terrible for him and asked if I could help in any way—order him some groceries, some dinner?

"Nah, haven't been able to eat much between the throat and the vomiting so no need to waste $$$. Not even water will stay down, just comes up, I keep trying though."

"Try ice chips maybe?" (I knew that dehydration can be serious, especially if you're by yourself; delirium can set in.)

He said he'd try that and added that he didn't have any chest pain or shortness of breath, which was a good sign, so he was not considered high risk.

"It's all temporary, not worried, I just gotta see it through and do my part"

"Jesus, u have a good attitude," I texted, "well I'm here if u need anything"

"Thank u, trust me I want my health restored"

"It will, u will"

When I checked back in with Mark a week later, he said he was feeling well, almost back to himself.

A Kiss at the Farmers Market
April 11, 2020

5 3

"I've got a present for you," Jesse texts me out of the blue. "Okay if I drop it off? I'm not far."

"Aww really? Yeah for sure"

I scrambled and found something small but perfect from my apartment as a gift in return. I left it for him at the front desk.

Jesse called as he was approaching the building. I could see him from a block away in his Carhartt jacket and cap. I opened my window and he stood on the sidewalk below, his mask pulled down, and we talked for a bit. Without traffic, the acoustics were perfect. It was nice to see his face, and that smile, even with eight stories between us. I wished I could tell him to come up. I'd give him a haircut. His hair was longer than I'd ever seen it.

"I know, I know," he said, boyishly rubbing a hand through it.

It sure was a sweet moment in the midst of all this. I blew a kiss when I said goodbye. I closed the window, put on my gloves, and dashed down the stairs to pick up my present.

Older Man in the Shade—Chinatown
May 30, 2020

5 4

Two or three summers ago, I was on Fourteenth Street near Fifth Avenue when I spotted a striking young woman wearing a long, high-collared dress. She had close-set eyes and pulled-back hair. I think she was a Jehovah's Witness.

"Instead of taking a picture of me, why don't you accept Jesus in your heart?" she said after I'd asked permission to take her photo.

I put down my camera.

"Maybe I already have," I replied with an easygoing smile, "maybe I already have accepted him in my heart."

She looked like she did not know what to say back to that.

"Is Jesus love?" I asked her.

"Yes."

"Well, there you are."

55

Deaths in New York passed fifteen thousand yesterday, the same day I met Nellie, a grounds caretaker at the public housing complex in Chelsea, five or six blocks from my place. I'd gone out for a walk with my camera around three o'clock and saw her sitting in her truck in an empty lot, staring into space, lost in thought. I didn't want to startle her.

"Hi, how're you doing?" I asked in a quiet voice.

"Tired."

"I'll bet."

"Fifteen days in a row," she said.

"Working—fifteen days without a day off?"

She nodded.

"Are you gonna get one?"

"Tuesday—supposed to get Tuesday off."

"Oh, man, thank you for doing what you're doing, being out, working," I said. "I'm sure this is hard—beyond what I can imagine."

Nellie nodded, look down, started to get a little choked up.

"I lost my partner on Wednesday—my work partner." She glanced at the empty seat next to her, where, I imagined, her partner would normally be.

Nellie shook her head, as if trying to figure something out, something that did not make sense. "He was only forty-two, healthy—strong! Just—gone—just—"

I didn't know what to say except for the only thing I could manage to say—that I was sorry, so sorry.

Nellie nodded.

"And how are you doing? How is your family?"

"Everyone's fine, everyone's healthy—thank the Lord."

"Yes, yes . . ."

"Thank the Lord," Nellie said.

Nellie, Caretaker, Fulton Houses
April 19, 2020

5 6

For the first time in the New York City subway system's 115-year history, the trains will not operate around the clock. Subway service on all lines will halt from one A.M. to five A.M. every day starting today so trains can be disinfected by workers.

When I heard this, the immediate image that came to my mind was of open-heart surgery—something I had the opportunity to witness once, a fascinating but grisly procedure that takes several hours: the patient's heart is stopped temporarily (its functions taken over by a machine) while life-saving repairs are done to damaged arteries. I knew then as I know now, it's precisely what *has* to be done, but there's something unsettling about it at the same time: the idea that you can remain alive, technically, without your *actual* heart beating. It might be fixed once it's restarted—as good as new or better—or it might not. You might never recover fully. You might never wake up.

5 7

Three subway scenes from before stay with me:

A young mother accidentally drops a baby toy as she carries an infant plus a bulky stroller up a crowded stairway at rush hour. The toy finally lands on a bottom step. Without a word, at least four people dash so fast to pick it up for her you'd almost think it was a pile of money. Kindnesses are palpable.

———————

A construction guy sneezes on the platform across the tracks. Someone on my side calls out "Bless you," and he tips his helmet in return.

———————

A tall man gets on at Wall Street and sits on the opposite bench. He sees me studying my piano flash cards—I'm still trying to memorize all the notes—and he asks about them. He tells me he played piano throughout his childhood in Costa Rica—his mother made him.

Now he works for a bank. "I wish I hadn't stopped," he says ruefully. He has long fingers, so unlike my stubby ones, and I imagine that he might have been a good pianist.

He notices the camera slung over my shoulder.

"Let me take your picture," I say spontaneously, "a portrait."

It takes a little bit of persuading, but eventually he agrees.

We get off at my stop and walk the few short blocks to my apartment. The sitting is very quick—fewer than ten minutes. He has to get home to his wife and kids.

"I never do things like this," he tells me as he leaves.

"Then why did you?"

"Because I never do things like this," he says.

Man from the Subway
June 15, 2015

5 8

"Have you ever climbed a mountain?" Oliver suddenly asks, apropos of nothing, as we lie in bed.

It's a drowsy afternoon ten years ago, not long after we'd gotten together.

I think about it, trying hard to remember, and the answer seems to suggest everything I've missed, have yet to do, have put off, in my life.

"No, I never have—never climbed one."

"You should. At my age, I don't regret the things I've done but those I haven't. I'm like a criminal in that way."

I kiss him on the forehead.

"I'm going to try to remember that, you old crook."

Panic/Don't Panic
April 14, 2020

59

The U.S. has now surpassed more than 1.5 million known corona-virus cases, and at least 100,000 people have died. More than a third of these deaths have been among nursing home residents and workers. Yesterday, I learned that my late partner Steve's mother, Millie, died from Covid-19 at the nursing home where she lived in Maryland.

The news locally is both terrible and encouraging: Daily deaths in New York have fallen below 100, the lowest figure since the end of March, and the numbers overall are gradually going down. Even so: approximately 100 people a day are still dying from this virus. At least 30,000 New Yorkers have died so far.

I remember when it was only one person—just a couple of months ago.

We are obviously a long way from returning to any semblance of normalcy. The lockdown that was supposed to end in New York by mid-May has been extended into June, and, like everyone, I am climbing the walls here. But I also know I am among the most fortu-nate: I have a roof over my head, food in my fridge, and my health to be thankful for. So, if this is how we have to live—with masks and gloves and almost no human contact for several more months—then so be it, this is how we have to live. I want to see what's on the other side of this fucking mountain.

6 0

Because what *is* is what matters most. What was will only make you blue in New York.

6 1

Today @ 3:04 P.M.
I get a text from Jesse:

"Babe"
"Babe," I reply.
"Had a dream about you lol"
"Yeah? What do you remember?"
"Laughing and fucking"
"That sounds like us"
"I legitimately woke up laughing"
"I love hearing that"
"I loved feeling it"
"I wish I could have that dream," I say.

Young Man with a Trumpet
April 30, 2020

POSTSCRIPT

In early March, when Covid-19 was the viral equivalent of a tsunami approaching, I started making notes about what I was seeing, hearing, feeling—noticing. This book soon began to take shape, and I wrote and photographed it in fewer than eight weeks. I aimed to provide a snapshot in real time of the early days of this crisis, and to preserve memories of a New York I saw rapidly disappearing.

Already, those early days—how we lived a mere two or three months ago—seem like distant memories. As I write this, the nation is in the throes of a long-overdue reckoning with our country's systemic racism, ignited by the latest killing of a Black person by white people: the brutal public torture and murder of George Floyd by Minneapolis police officers on May 25.

Just a few weeks ago, it was so quiet I could hear from my apartment birds singing and trees rustling. Yet right now I am surrounded by noise I can't shut out by closing windows and doors: helicopters circling; sirens wailing; horns honking at the gas station as people fill up before the eight P.M. curfew; table saws cutting plywood to protect shop windows from looters; and gloriously, raucously loud protesters—most masked, some not—chanting as they march up Eighth Avenue by the thousands, blocking traffic on Fourteenth Street: "Whose Streets? *Our* Streets!" "Justice *Now*!" "Black Lives *Matter*! Black Lives *Matter*! Black Lives *Matter*!"

Suddenly, police are everywhere—on bikes, on foot, carrying batons and zip ties.

My eyes fill with tears, and I send a text to Jesse: "YOU matter to me—I hope you know that."

"I love you," he texts back.

I grab my camera, put on a face mask, stuff an extra one plus hand sanitizer into a pocket, and head out the door to bear witness. Curfew starts in just a few hours.

—June 3, 2020
New York City

ACKNOWLEDGMENTS

Thank you:
Zann Erick
Emily Forland
Emma Hopkin
Tara Kennedy
Myunghee Kwon
Cindy Loh
Nancy Miller
Laura Phillips
Patti Ratchford

A NOTE ON THE AUTHOR

BILL HAYES is the author of *Insomniac City* and *The Anatomist*, among other books, and a forthcoming history of exercise, *Sweat*, to be published by Bloomsbury in 2021. Hayes is a recipient of a Guggenheim Fellowship in nonfiction and is a frequent contributor to the *New York Times*. A collection of his street photography, *How New York Breaks Your Heart*, was published recently by Bloomsbury. Hayes has completed the screenplay for a film adaptation of *Insomniac City*, currently in the works from Hopscotch Features, and he is a co-editor of Oliver Sacks's posthumous books. He lives in New York. Visit his website at billhayes.com.